Old ABERDOUR

by

J. A. Kennedy

The publishers regret that they cannot supply
copies of any pictures featured in this book.

ACKNOWLEDGEMENTS

My grateful thanks must be recorded to Ian Brodie, Alan Brotchie, Bill
Lynn, Eric Simpson, Ian Stevens and John Taylor.

INTRODUCTION

In his contribution to the *Statistical Account of Scotland* (1790), the Revd Robert Liston described the inhabitants of Aberdour (then numbering 840 souls) as follows: '[They are] sober and industrious, are contented with their situation, enjoy in a considerable degree the advantages of society, and while in health they are able to maintain their families. In sickness and old age many need relief. . . . To improve the condition of the people, care should be taken to improve their morals.' Who could possibly disagree with these sentiments, or fail to agree that with the passage of more than 200 years Revd Liston's hopes for improvement have come to pass? Today's village has grown to a population of 1,690 (at the time of the census in the year 2000), but of which probably only a very small percentage now actually earn their income locally. As a vibrant commuting village for Edinburgh, Aberdour has many attractions, its compact and distinct character benefiting significantly from a regular rail service to the capital.

The present village is an agglomeration of three separate elements. The oldest of these, Easter Aberdour, grew up around the twelfth-century castle, the ancient seat of the de Mortimers, then the Douglases (Earls of Morton from 1458). Wester Aberdour, the second settlement, was an ancient burgh of barony under the jurisdiction of the Abbot of Inchcolm Priory, which later formed part of the estate of the Earl of Moray. The third part, the 'Newtown', located south of the older areas and closer to the harbour, was largely a product of the nineteenth century tourist trade.

Aberdour's harbour was served by a regular ferry to Leith or Granton, and was also used for the shipping of coal. In 1861 it was recorded that 'as many as twenty-five vessels of . . . up to 200 tons burden . . . have been crowded into it at one time. The principal article of export is coal, of which 150,000 tons have been exported in one year by the Donibristle Coal Coy. The imports are small, the chief article being manure for the farmers of the district.' The only other local industry was weaving by hand loom to produce coarse cloth.

Coal exports ceased in 1871 (rail transport having superseded sailing vessels), but by then the nature of the 'goods' imported had also changed radically, with the little port acting as a magnet for large numbers of visitors arriving by steamship. Many wealthy Edinburgh businessmen despatched their families (and servants) to the large new villas of Newtown for the summer, with the head of the family joining them at weekends. These temporary incomers were supplemented by hundreds of day trippers, catered for mostly by steamers of the Galloway fleet, whose proprietor, M. P. Galloway, had built for his family's use the isolated Forth View House (see pages 44 and 45) at Hawkcraig Point next to his wooden low-water pier. Around this time there were no fewer than 24 registered lodging houses, plus several hotels, while 'a number of parties let out one or two rooms during the season'. The pretty village with its sandy beaches and stunning views across the Firth of Forth to Edinburgh became 'a favourite retreat to the inhabitants of the Scottish capital, who there seek relaxation and leisure during the heats of summer'.

More visitors of the same type arrived by train following the opening of the rail bridge over the Forth at Queensferry in 1890 and the simultaneous establishment of a station in Aberdour close to the castle. This involved the diversion of the road between Easter and Wester Aberdour, plus relocation of the castle's north gateway. Aberdour Station is one of the gems of the rail network to this day, with well-tended flower beds and hanging baskets.

Services at Aberdour's ancient church, one of the best examples of Norman architecture in Scotland, are well-attended. A church is known to have been in existence on this site in 1123, but fell into ruin after the roof was removed in 1796. Through the generosity of the Misses Laurie of Starley the ruin was restored as a place of worship in 1925–6, being rededicated on 7 July 1926.

An up-to-date and comprehensive history of the village is long overdue. This small booklet is not designed to fulfil this role, but if it stimulates that end it will have achieved one of its goals. The Revd William Ross published his *Aberdour and Inchcolme* (sic) in 1885, but unsurprisingly a large proportion of its 396 pages is given over to ecclesiastical matters. Subsequent histories have mostly dealt with specific topics (the church, golf club, post office, railway station), and while excellent in their own way they merely serve to whet the appetite for the 'full story'. Perhaps somebody will now grasp the nettle.

It is entirely possible that sufficient material of interest may exist for a second volume of *Old Aberdour*. If you think that you could help with this, please contact the publisher.

Opposite: The massive proportions of Seabank House, with its central chimney cluster, are seen to advantage in this 1937 view. The house passed from the Hendersons to the Calderwood-Durham family, who sold it prior to 1910, after which it became the Seabank Hotel, serving as such for some years until eventually returning to domestic use. Also designed by the same renowned architect, Thomas Hamilton, were Kinghorn School (now the community centre) and Kennoway Parish Church.

The attractions of Aberdour to the Victorians were not merely scenic: travel to the seaside village from Leith bestowed upon the thirsty the status of 'bona fide traveller', allowing them to meet the then regulatory requirement of having made a journey of more than three miles and thus enabling them to purchase alcoholic refreshment! The law was manipulated in many ways, all to the advantage of the many inns located providentially at just this precise distance beyond the boundaries of Scotland's towns and cities. Aberdour thus became the destination of many excursion and pleasure boat sailings from Leith, with a consequent influx of merrymakers to the village, some sober when they arrived, a smaller number so when leaving. This view from the Hawkcraig shows the Galloway Company's steamer *Tantallon Castle* in 1890, just three years after being put into service. She was a regular visitor until 1898, thereafter plying the sunnier waters of the Bosporus.

A good idea of the numbers of visitors who could descend on Aberdour is given by this late Victorian photograph. Taken on the same occasion as the picture on page 9 of Ian Brodie's *Steamers of the Forth, Volume 2* (www.stenlake.co.uk), most of these passengers have just disembarked from the *Fiery Cross*, owned by George Jamieson until his death in 1893. On the left are two steam yachts, with another alongside the quay in the foreground.

Here the photographer has turned his camera 180° to look east from the same vantage point as the previous picture. Passengers from the steamers standing off the harbour are sampling the pleasures of a stroll along the 'promenade' leading to the foot of Shore Road. The levelled area here was created from the ballast of sailing ships arriving at the harbour to load coal from Lord Morton's Donibristle Colliery. It may come as a surprise to some to learn that the picturesque harbour was used for the export of coal until 1871. Chinese lanterns were strung among the trees during the annual Aberdour Regatta.

The *Fair Maid* at Aberdour's stone pier, probably in 1937, the final summer of operation of regular steamers to and from the small harbour. At the commencement of the Second World War shipping on the River Forth was curtailed on the orders of the Admiralty. The *Fair Maid* was built in Ayr in 1886 as the *Madge Wildfire* and was renamed *Isle of Skye* in 1913, plying the Clyde excursion traffic before being transferred to the Forth in 1927. Here the harbour is well filled with small vessels, some of which look as if they have been adapted as houseboats, with one sporting a line of washing hung out to dry! At this time the wooden pier, which the *Fair Maid* had permission to use at low tide, was still usable. It is seen beyond the stern of the vessel.

In 1956 the harbour presented a tranquil appearance when viewed from the Ladies' Walk footpath below Hawkcraig, as indeed it still does. Most of the old wooden vessels in the previous picture had gone by this date, but two or three working fishing boats can be seen tied up alongside. Evidence of fishing activities can also be seen in the large number of lobster pots stacked at the pierhead. Lobster and crab fishing continued on a reduced scale into the 1990s, the last boat being Willie Rutherford's *Summer Rose*. Seabank House can be seen in the centre of the photograph, at the foot of Shore Road.

A busy day on the Black Sands in the mid-1930s. In contrast with the White Sands on the eastern side of Hawkcraig Point, the beach here seems to have picked up coal debris from the collieries of Dysart and Wemyss some miles away to the east which deposited their waste directly into the sea. Even today such traces of coal still wash up here. Features of the Aberdour scene then were the small motor boats that plied to the island of Inchcolm some one and a half miles offshore; the nearer one in this view is the *St Joan*. Unfortunately there are now no regular excursions to the island from the village, the last having been operated by Dougal Barrie in the mid-1980s.

In the 1950s the Anstruther lifeboat, RNLB *James and Ruby Jackson*, was on hand during the Aberdour Regatta. This vessel of the Liverpool class was funded by a legacy from James Jackson of Falkland and served from 1950 to 1965, helping to save 45 lives. Aberdour maintains close links with the RNLI, whose volunteers still usually provide a stall at the annual regatta.

Opposite: As visitors walked from the harbour up Shore Road towards the centre of the village they came to Seaside Place, seen here in the late 1920s. The three-storey tenement on the left towards the end of the street is reputedly the oldest in this part of the village, built to accommodate workers on the Earl of Moray's estate. On the horizon, behind the second house on the left, the obelisk on Cuttlehill can be made out. This was erected for the 13th Earl of Morton in 1744 to enable him to see this boundary of his estate from his seat at Dalmahoy in Midlothian.

Seaside Place looking west towards the entrance to the golf course at the far end of the street. On the left is Pringle's garage, complete with its hand-cranked Pratt's petrol pump. The site is now occupied by a modern house, as are all other suitable sites which were then vacant. Beyond the garage is a large house, constructed at the same period and in similar architectural style to Seabank House. When the photograph was taken the street was lit by gas lamps, supplied from the village's small gasworks behind St Colme's Crescent. The road was then surfaced with water-bound macadam, and although Seaside Place has still not been adopted by the local authority it does at least now have a tarred surface.

Clachaig House (a boarding house at the time the previous view of Seaside Place was taken) is a handsome Victorian 'B'-listed villa which merits a mention in the Fife volume of *The Buildings of Scotland*. Attention is drawn to its 'superimposed orders (Corinthian above Doric)' which are shown to good effect in this study. Unfortunately the ornate cast-iron gates and garden railings were removed in the ill-advised Second World War scrap metal drive, but the window-box guards remain. For many years Clachaig House was the residence of Mrs Alison A. Buckle, whose maids stand by the front door in this picture. Minnie Smith, right, later ran the local fruiterer's shop, while Mary Dalgliesh, left, married Tom Milne, the Aberdour baker. In the left foreground is a cast-iron water fountain.

Parallel to and north of Seaside Place runs Manse Street, seen here in 1915. Lined on both sides by attractive (but probably then quite basic) white-painted two-storey cottages, it retains its air of tranquillity, and still even has the roses growing around the doors! The manse at the west end of the street dates from 1802 and was designed by the architect Robert Burn. In 1996–7 it was reconstructed as flats, with the replacement manse now at 36 Bellhouse Road.

The picturesque footbridge over the Dour Burn where it enters Aberdour harbour. Behind, overlooking the fields, are the houses of Home Park. Fortunately development here has been prevented so far, allowing the character of the little glen to remain unspoiled for the enjoyment of all. The large double house to the extreme top right is of a style which has been described as 'Seaside Art Nouveau'. It was newly completed when the scene was recorded in 1909.

A 1909 view looking over the public park (the former official name being Coalfauld Park) from Shore Road. Aberdour's Park Lane (background) developed from west to east (left to right as seen). The first house to be built, Straith Villa, bears the date 1872 and the unusual balconied design of the later houses was to be repeated elsewhere in the village. Within the park a fun fair has been set up, with roundabouts, a small swing-boat and the showman's horse-drawn caravan. The bowling green is receiving the attention of the groundsman and his heavy roller. The corner where the green was established in 1891 had served until twenty years previously as a yard where coal was stored prior to shipping, the cottage on the corner of Shore Road and Park Lane bearing the name 'Caulfield' to this day. The trees parallel to Shore Road were donated by local businessmen.

The children's play area in the public park has been remodelled since this busy 1950s photograph was taken and is due to undergo another transformation soon. Although the tennis courts were well-established by this date, the present clubhouse is conspicuous by its absence. Since the photograph was taken the clay courts have been replaced by an all-weather surface, and with floodlighting also installed it is now not unusual to see tennis being played in the depths of winter.

Looking north up Shore Road from Park Lane in 1905. Kinnaird's Temperance Hotel and Tea Gardens on the left were a favourite stop for excursionists, the establishment priding itself on its temperance status and putting great emphasis on *tea*. The Aberdour Institute and local library now occupy this site. Opposite is one of Aberdour's several hotels – then John McLauchlan's 'Star' (despite the large golden lion visible above the front door) – but now much better known as the popular Cedar Inn. The pierrot figure on the left has escaped from his seaside stage, perhaps to lure customers from Kinnaird's.

The overpowering but magical interior of Kinnaird's Tea Gardens on Shore Road. An incredible collection of porcelain busts, figurines and pot plants contrasts starkly with bare trestle tables and benches! Note the hammocks slung from the roof joists. These weren't just for a touch of character, but provided overnight accommodation at a cost of 9*d*., excluding breakfast. A two-course dinner cost 1*s*. 3*d*. It is believed that the seated figure to the extreme right was the proprietor, William Kinnaird, 'confectioner of Leith', himself. This photograph was used in brochures advertising his establishment.

The 18th green of Aberdour golf course in 1909, with the original clubhouse behind, and the gate to Seaside Place firmly closed. The club was founded as a 9-hole course at Couston (to the west of the village) in 1896, moving to its current location in 1905 and being extended to 18 holes in 1914. It was a condition of the initial lease that 'no player was allowed access to the Avenue [to St Colme's House] to search for a lost ball'. During the Second World War the course reverted to 9 holes, with the area nearest the shore being occupied by gun emplacements manned by detachments of the Polish army.

A previous configuration of the course (before the ground for the final extension was obtained from Shell–Esso) is seen in this August 1938 view looking down on the 10th (Cottage) hole and 11th tee alongside the beach. Now the 3rd hole is by the wall, with the 4th returning towards the cottage, the direction of play having been reversed. George Todd occupied Kinniker Cottage here by the shore of Port Haven Bay. It had no road access whatsoever, and became derelict after 1970, finally being demolished in 1977. Much of the prominent Bellhouse Rock on the ness to the right collapsed during the winter of 1999/2000.

Competition to Kinnaird's was typified by Milner's Tea Garden, located off Aberdour High Street. It was situated behind Mrs Taddei's ice cream shop, later the co-op and general store and recently a small plant nursery. Mr Milner may be the aproned figure standing on the left, while beside him is a remarkable display of 'MD Finest Briars' (pipes, to the uninitiated). Milner also did a steady business in picture postcards, including this one featuring his own business.

The High Street looking west in 1909. Milner's Tea Garden was behind the first white painted building on the left. Shortly after this photograph was taken, this was converted into a combined tobacconist's, electrician's and radio agent's. The gap beyond Wotherspoon's confectionery shop was soon to be filled by a single-storey cafe, which was replaced by a two-storey ice cream parlour with a stylish 1930s frontage that is now home to the village general store. Note the porters' barrows, no doubt in great demand for transporting luggage from the station to holiday residences. It was then the habit to send a trunk (or two) in advance of the holiday party so that travellers did not have to be encumbered. There is not much opportunity today for dogs to lie peacefully in the middle of the street!

The same end of the High Street, this time looking east in 1915. The shops are, from the left, Downie's grocer's, McLaren's bazaar, Seath's Golf Restaurant and Walter Crow's plumber's. Niven's butcher's shop occupies the prominent site at the corner of Shore Road. The closure of the butcher's in 1996, partly due to the presence of nearby supermarkets, was a major loss, the still-empty shop casting an unfortunate blight on the centre of the village. When the photograph was taken the Dr Spence memorial clock was in its original position (just out of shot to the left), with its present site at the station entrance vacant.

An early twentieth century view of the Established Church dating from before the erection of the Spence clock. When originally planned the church was to face directly down Shore Road, but for some reason it was built slightly further to the west. Completed in 1790, it was of the same design as another at Dyke near Forres, again on the Earl of Moray's estates. After the reconsecration of St Fillan's in 1926, it assumed the role of church hall. The notices beside the entrance gates include an advert for the regatta and an army recruiting poster. A memorial honouring the men from the parish who died in subsequent wars was later added on the south wall of the church. The postcard was sent in July 1906.

This picture of the High Street poses a minor mystery. According to the photographer's records it was taken in the summer of 1909, but the Spence memorial clock, supposedly commissioned in 1910, is already in place on its pediment on the church wall! The lads posing below the clock are members of the Crow family, long-time 'keepers of the clock' with its routine maintenance in their hands for many years. The Spence clock was erected by local people as a lasting memorial to their 'Friend and Physician for nearly 40 years'. In later years the wall in front of the church was reduced in height to allow sight of the war memorial.

In August 1904 the sender of this postcard of Aberdour High Street was 'having fair weather upon the whole', but summers then always seemed to be blessed with fine weather (at least in the memory). Several windows have boards advertising rooms to let. The old outside stairs, once a familiar sight, have long gone from this part of the High Street although one or two examples remain in other corners.

45911 Aberdour, Woodside Hotel &c F&Co.

Greig's well-known Woodside Hotel in its original (1880) extent, with, on the far side, the post office, occupying the site of the later Doune Hall. This hall, used as the village institute and by the YMCA, was a bequest to the village from the Hon. Wm J. Hewitt of St Colme's House, the Earl of Moray's factor, in memory of his two sons who died in the First World War. The hall is now incorporated into the hotel, as is the other old building flanking it to the west. One of the most notable features of the hotel is the richly decorated lantern-roofed state room from the Orient Line's RMS *Orontes*, bought and installed as a bar behind the hotel when it was being broken up at Inverkeithing in 1926.

Facing the Woodside Hotel are the decorative cast-iron gates and 'B'-listed east lodge of Donibristle House. The gates date from 1870, and along with an identical set at Darnaway Castle near Forres were gifted by estate workers. Unfortunately the central gates are no longer in place at Aberdour, it being believed that they were sent to Darnaway to replace the others which had decayed. Public access to the estate was once restricted to Tuesdays and Fridays only, but now users of the Fife Coastal Path (the section to Dalgety Bay starts here) enjoy unrestricted access. The avenue is particularly notable for its spring display of daffodils. At the end of the bulb season each year, all bulbs unsold by a Kirkcaldy merchant were planted on the Donibristle drive to create a spectacle which is still greatly appreciated. Such is the profusion of flowers that bunches are sold to benefit Cancer Research UK, with several hundred pounds raised by volunteers each year.

The station entrance seen in the period between 1919 – when the Spence Clock was moved here – and 1923, when the North British Railway was absorbed into the London & North Eastern Railway. The phone box is one of the very earliest concrete types which were replaced by the better-known and award-winning Gilbert Scott red cast-iron style kiosk. Aberdour retains its red phone box, still in this location. On the extreme right is the entrance to Aberdour House.

Aberdour House was built in the 1600s as a more comfortable home for the Earl of Morton than Aberdour Castle. It was remodelled several times over the centuries, and during the First World War was used as the official residence of Admiral Beatty, commander of Rosyth Naval Base and eventually in complete control of the Grand Fleet of the British Navy. While in residence here Admiral Beatty was visited on 17 June 1916 by King George V, who disembarked at the harbour and walked up through the fields to the house. Aberdour House was converted into flats in 1988–90, with modern homes to a sympathetic design built in the grounds. On the right is the famous sundial, dating from 1640, which has now been restored to its former position at the castle. The picture dates from 1905.

Aberdour Castle.

Aberdour Castle is one of the major attractions in a village rich in historical interest, the earliest remaining parts of it dating back to the twelfth century. The castle remained the property of the Douglas family (Earls of Morton from 1458) after they built Aberdour House, but was severely damaged by fire in the seventeenth century and was then basically left as a ruin which was probably used as a convenient source of stone for other local buildings. Major sections collapsed in 1844 and 1919 leading to care of the remaining structure being placed in the custody of the Secretary of State for Scotland. When this postcard was produced the castle ruins included a hen run (foreground)!

In *The Buildings of Scotland*, St Fillan's is described as 'a friendly little church in a comfortable graveyard beside Aberdour Castle'. The same authority dates the founding of the church here to *c*.1140, although the date 1123 has long been accepted for its foundation. Either way, it is one of the oldest ecclesiastical structures in Scotland, and certainly one of the earliest which is still in regular use. It is a simple, atmospheric place of worship, rightly dubbed 'a cathedral in miniature'. The roof was removed in 1796 and the remains of the building were almost demolished at that time.

When, in 1914, the ministry of Aberdour Parish was entrusted to the Revd Robert Johnstone he had the vision of reconstructing and rededicating the ruin that had been St Fillan's Church. Eventually several benefactors raised the necessary amount for the work to begin; chief among these were the sisters I. E. M. and C. A. Laurie of Starley. Kirkcaldy architect William Williamson was appointed to design and supervise the works. The newly reconstructed building is seen in this photograph, with the castle on the left above the entry porch. Revd Dr Johnstone enjoyed the fruits of his efforts, serving in the restored church until his retirement in 1940.

Restoration took less than a year, and this interior view was probably recorded shortly after the church's rededication by the Moderator of the General Assembly of the Church of Scotland on 7 July 1926. Masonry work was carried out by W. & A. Moyes of Aberdour, with the highly praised woodwork undertaken by local joiners, the brothers Lyon. To the right of the pulpit can be seen the original baptismal font, found lying in the churchyard and reinstalled on a new stone base. The charming 'mini-cathedral' is open daily to visitors, and is a blaze of flowers during the annual Aberdour Festival.

Aberdour Station was built by the North British Railway and opened on 2 June 1890 as part of the work associated with the new railway bridge over the River Forth. The line thereafter formed part of the main route between Edinburgh and Aberdeen and saw a continuous flow of traffic of all types, from through expresses to stopping passenger locals, express fish trains and mineral traffic. Given the scale of traffic *then* being carried, it seems impossible to believe that the rail network is currently operating at capacity. This busy scene was photographed on 21 August 1911 and shows a long troop-carrying train heading south hauled by NBR 'Scott' class No. 900, the *Fair Maid*, and a mineral train, probably from one of the west Fife pits, making for Burntisland with a cargo destined for shipping overseas.

The two photographs on this page were taken just days apart by the late G. M. Shoults, who was probably then holidaying in the village. Heading south on this occasion is the 1.20 p.m. Aberdeen to Edinburgh express, hauled by one of the NBR's impressive 'Atlantic' class locomotives, No. 874, *Dunedin*. Worthy of note is the first coach, noticeably different from the others. This was owned by the Great North of Scotland Railway and operated as a through coach from Elgin to Edinburgh, a journey then of some six and a half hours.

Hillside House has had a chequered history. Built early in the nineteenth century on the site of an earlier mansion, it was the home of the Wotherspoon family from 1856 to 1934. It then came into the possession of three successive orders of nuns, and at the time of this photograph, *c*.1938, was known as St Teresa's Holiday Home. During the Second World War the building was occupied by the armed forces, as were many others. From 1960 it was used by the Salesian Fathers of St John Bosco as a 'List D' school and is now Hillside residential special school, with accommodation for up to 35 boys. Several utilitarian structures were added around the original building in 1969, which lost its sense of presence in consequence. Hillside House was recorded as a favourite haunt of James Hogg, the 'Ettrick Shepherd'.

Until the middle of the last century Easter Aberdour had a fair number of early two-storey cottages, but very few examples of these remain. There were then no openings leading north, and to allow development of the Glebe some old buildings were removed to make way for Murrell Road and Murrell Terrace. The nearer stone buildings in this picture date from the Victorian era. Milne Terrace was built speculatively by Tom Milne the baker.

Main Street, Easter Aberdour, prior to the First World War. The street has changed little in appearance today, although volumes of traffic are greater. To the right is the Railway Inn, later the Drift Inn but now converted to domestic use. On the rear dividing wall between Nos 13 and 15 Main Street sits an unusual carved stone piper. One of Aberdour's oldest dwelling houses is Templeland, the white-painted building with crow-stepped gables, built on ground owned in the Middle Ages by the Knights Templar. For many years it was the home of the county roadman.

A 1956 photograph taken from behind the post-war council houses of Cullaloe Crescent. The scene encompasses many of Aberdour's attractions, particularly the stunning panorama across the Forth to Inchcolm, Edinburgh and the Pentland Hills. Aberdour Church nestles among the trees in the centre of the view.

Inchcolm Abbey lies within Aberdour Parish, and is often described as the Iona of the east. The island of Inchcolm is not now accessible by a regular boat from Aberdour but can be reached from South Queensferry. Its abbey is the best preserved monastic settlement in Scotland, with the Augustinian monastery one of several founded in Fife in the twelfth century by Scotland's pious King David I. The abbey was abandoned at the time of the Reformation in 1560 and allowed to fall into ruin. Inchcolm's strategic position in the Forth ensured that it was fortified, with a gun battery constructed at the end of the eighteenth century to protect against Napoleon's anticipated invasion. Later additions to the defences were made in both the First and Second World Wars. From 1924 the entire island was put under the care of the Secretary of State and is now administered by Historic Scotland. The translation of a carved stone above the entrance is 'May this house stand until an ant drains the flowing sea and a tortoise walks around the whole world'.

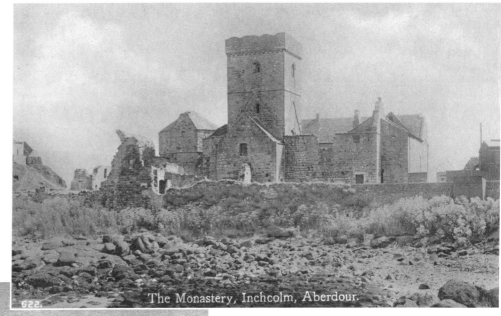

The Monastery, Inchcolm, Aberdour.

Easter Aberdour looking north along Hawkcraig Road to the 'old town'. The primary school now occupies the field on the right. Barely discernible is the railway cutting just on this side of the houses. There were no houses on the left here until the bungalows overlooking Home Park were built between 1948 and 1952 by Colin Morris of Inverkeithing. The road saw considerable traffic from the whinstone quarries developed at Hawkcraig, initially by the Carlingnose Granite Co. of North Queensferry.

The east sands, formerly known as the White Sands but now 'rebranded' as the Silver Sands, draw hundreds on fine summer weekends, most now arriving by private car. One of Aberdour's acclaimed blue flag beaches, it never seems to be blighted by coal debris and has always been a magnet for bathers on the few hot days of summer.

A summer afternoon at the Silver Sands in the early 1950s. For a short time there was a miniature railway at the east side of the bay, adding to the natural attractions.

The Beach Cafe at the Silver Sands, with its brightly striped umbrellas on the terrace, attempted to bring a Mediterranean atmosphere to the bay. Taken on the same sunny day as the previous view, the cafe was well-patronised during good weather. In recent times it has assumed a new lease of life as The Swell, a surfing themed cafe!

A 1930s view taken at the western end of the Silver Sands showing a coaster loading stone at the quarry company's pier. A narrow-gauge tramway linked the quarry to the pier using horsepower. The remains of the short pier can be seen at the east side of the recently reconstructed offices here (formerly home to a small boat-building yard).

The quarries on the Hawkcraig created extensive excavations which were rapidly filled in during the 1950s as receptacles for household rubbish. Today it is difficult to imagine this industrial scene of not so many years ago. Most of the excavated stone was used as road metal. Here the tram line to the pier is being covered in; afterwards it ran through a tunnel here.

The crusher at the quarry was belt-driven by this traction engine. The engine was then unyoked and pulled the stone in carts to a siding on the north side of the railway line. Here it would be shovelled into trucks for despatch onwards. The sloping wooden shelter was built to protect the traction engine from flying debris when the quarry was blasting.

A little-known facet of Aberdour's history involves the part played from 1915–18 by HMS *Tarlair*, the official title of the experimental station at Hawkcraig Point. All that remains today of this station where over 600 ratings and 100 officers conducted important experiments into 'hydrophones' are some undistinguished concrete bases. A series of articles in the Aberdour *Village News* by Diana Maxwell has comprehensive details of this remarkable enterprise. Hydrophones were underwater listening devices, the development of which led to sightings of over 50 German U-boats and several sinkings.

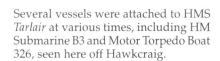

Several vessels were attached to HMS *Tarlair* at various times, including HM Submarine B3 and Motor Torpedo Boat 326, seen here off Hawkcraig.

Tarlair's chippies, from the left Petty Officers W. Lyon, unknown, McClinchey and McLauchlan. Is it just coincidence that these are well-known Aberdour names, or were local men occasionally kept close to home?

The *Wemyss Castle* lies at the wooden pier at low tide in the summer of 1905. This pier was opened about 1870 and enabled landings to be made at all states of the tide. The pathway on the seaward side of the cottages no longer exists and the building advertising 'Ice Cream & Refreshments' has been incorporated into a private house. Behind can be seen the Forth View Hotel, with a sign (which it retains today) on the roof advertising its temperance status. Forth View was built by M. P. Galloway, one of the original proprietors of the steamship line of the same name, as his Fife residence.

Hawkcraig and Forth View Hotel, Aberdour. 4

The Forth View Hotel from the wooden pier, with the Hawkcraig cliffs behind. These are considered to be an ideal ascent for novice climbers, with permanently fitted metal pins and rings in place to assist them. The pier was used by the Admiralty during the First World War and also by the North British Railway, which inherited it from the Galloway Saloon Steam Packet Company. A tender for repair of the pier from Percy Trentham & Co. was accepted in 1921; the work was delayed, but carried out later. The Earl of Morton received a payment to allow the termination of Galloway's lease, this being the final step required before the Galloway company could be wound up. The wooden pier is now in ruins.

Otterston is a beauty spot close to Aberdour with several notable buildings situated round the banks of the attractive small loch. In the trees to the left can be seen Otterston House, which at one time was owned by the Hendersons of Fordel. In the right foreground are the ruins of Couston Castle where Rev'd Robert Blair, persecuted chaplain to King Charles I, obtained sanctuary in the seventeenth century.

A sylvan scene at the east end of Otterston Loch, which is still an oasis of tranquillity today, just off the beaten track. Out of shot, to the left of the photographer, is Cockairnie House, a former residence of the Moubrays dating from the mid-eighteenth century. It has an interesting older door lintel of 1589, inscribed 'welcvm.freindis'.

Balmule Farm, just north of Aberdour, was much used in the early years of the last century as a site for camps, particularly those of the Territorial Army. In 1909 the Royal Scots were photographed marching behind their fife and drum band, passing the cottages at Bernard's Smithy with Cullaloe Reservoir in the distance. That year there were more than 3,000 'Terriers' at the Balmule camp.

Royal Scott's arriving in camp, A b...

There must have been money to be made photographing these annual events, as the 'retreat' from camp was also covered. The cottages at Bernard's Smithy crossroads are seen in the background. The journey to and from Aberdour was often made by boat on a chartered steamer either from Leith or Granton. At weekends the camps played host to hundreds of visitors who watched the men on manoeuvres.

46.

9th. Royal Scots Marching out, Aberdour 19...